Sing, Mary!

by CAROLYN NYSTROM
Illustrated by Sheena Dawson

Text © 2004 Carolyn Nystrom
Illustrations © 2004 Angus Hudson Ltd/Tim Dowley &
Peter Wyart trading as Three's Company

Published in the USA by Kregel Publications 2004
Distributed by Kregel Publications,
Grand Rapids, Michigan 49501

Learn more about Mary in Matthew 1:18–2:23; Luke
1:18–25; 2:1–52; John 2:1–11; 19:16–27; and Acts
2:1–13.

ISBN 0-8254-3336-3

Worldwide co-edition produced by Lion Hudson plc,
Mayfield House, 256 Banbury Road,
Oxford OX2 7DH,
Tel: +44 (0) 1865 302750
Fax: +44 (0) 1865 302757
e-mail: coed@lionhudson.com
www.lionhudson.com

Printed in China

04 05 06 07 08 / 5 4 3 2 1

My first memories
are her strong arms around me
holding me close,
her warm milky smell, and
her soft voice singing.

I love you my baby, my sweet.
Be strong in my love.
You are mine,
a beautiful gift from God.

I nestled against my mother,
Anne, and slept.
My name is Mary.

3

I grew and played and sang
and grew some more.
I learned to sew and
I made clothing for my doll.
I rocked my doll and sang.
I prayed to God, as all my people prayed.
I prayed that Messiah would come.

When I was old enough to take a husband,
Joseph came and talked to my father.
My father said yes, Joseph could marry me.
Then Joseph went away
and I began to sew for my wedding.

4

5

Up down, up down, my needle stitched through blue cloth.
I hummed my sewing song.
Suddenly a shaft of light pierced the window.
My hands shook with fear.
"Don't be afraid," an angel said. "The Lord is with you."
My needle fell to the floor.
"You will have a baby,
and you must name him Jesus."
My hand flew to my belly.
"He will be a king who rules forever–the Messiah."

Now I was shaking all over.
"How can this be?" I asked.
"My baby won't have a father."
"Yes, he will," the angel smiled.
"He will be the Son of God."
Now I felt as calm as gentle rain.
"I am God's servant," I said.
"May God do all that you have said."

I needed a woman to talk to,
someone old and wise.
So I went to Aunt Elizabeth.

Her tummy was big and round.
She would have a baby, too!
And soon.
We laughed and hugged.

Then she looked into my eyes.
"God's Spirit speaks," she said.
"Blessed are you among women,
And blessed is the baby inside you.
You believe God will do
what he told you."

"Sing, Mary," I heard God's Spirit say.
I sang my praise to God.

My soul glorifies the Lord
and my spirit rejoices in God my Savior.
From now on all people will call me blessed,
for God has done great things for me.
His mercy reaches from age to age
for all who fear him.
God has helped his people,
just as he promised
our fathers.

Joseph told me what happened next.
"Mary already has a baby growing inside her,"
the people said. Joseph frowned.
He knew that he was not the daddy.

But an angel came to Joseph, too!
"Don't be afraid to make Mary your wife,"
the angel said. "God is the baby's father.
That baby is Immanuel, 'God is with us.'
He will save his people from their sins."

These were strange words,
hard to understand,
but Joseph listened.
"Take care of Mary," the angel said.
"Take care of her baby."
"I will," said Joseph.

Much later we traveled to Bethlehem.
My baby was big inside.
All day I rode a donkey.
I rode for days and days and days.
Each bump made my belly hurt.
Joseph led the way and watched for stones.
I did not sing that day.

In Bethlehem we found a place to rest.
There was no room inside where other people slept.
But we were warm and dry in a stable.
Beasts shuffled their feet
and breathed their snuffling sounds.
The smell of grain wrapped around us like a cloak.
The stars, like fire and ice, lit the sky.
That night God's Son was born.
Beyond the stars I heard an angel's song.
I held the baby and sang a lullaby to God.

I heard a whisper and a shuffling at the door.
A lamb cried, "*Ma-a-a-a.*"
A little boy crept in and peeked at baby Jesus.
The little shepherd's father, his uncle,
and a friend stood near
and leaned on shepherds' crooks.
They were amazed to see baby-God
lying still, asleep on the straw.

"We heard an angel sing," they said.
"And then a host of angels came.
The sky shone white with the light of angels,
their voices rose and sang
and shouted praise to God.
'Glory, Glory, Glory to God
in the highest,
and peace to his people on earth.'
We shook because we were afraid.
But the angels sent us here."

I wondered, *What does all this mean?*
The angel song? The peace on earth?
I held my baby, soft and small.
What lay ahead for me?
What lay ahead for him?

We took him to the temple
where our people worship God.
"What is his name?" they asked.
"His name is Jesus," we answered, full of joy.
"An angel told us."
Old Simeon held the baby high and sang.

Lord, my eyes now see your salvation
which you have given for all people of the earth.

Simeon put the baby back into my arms.
"Now I can die in peace," he said.

Old Anna stood in the shadows and prayed.
"Thank you, mighty God.
Your people have waited
all of history for this child."

Then Old Simeon looked at me.
His joyful eyes turned sad.
"You will have much hurt, my dear.
You will feel a sword cut through your heart."

I wondered what he meant—
but didn't want to know.

17

One night I watched the stars.
I saw one brighter than them all.
It seemed to move toward me—and him.

Soon dusty men came near.
"We've followed the star," they said.
"We've traveled months to find this place."
They knelt before my child and prayed.
(Did they know that he is God?)
They gave him gifts that only kings receive.
(Did they see him as a king?)

"Get up," an angel said, waking Joseph.
"King Herod will kill all baby boys.
Take Mary.
Take Jesus.
Run to Egypt."

"I will take care of them,"
my husband said.
We rode for weeks and weeks.

Much later, an angel spoke again to Joseph.
"It is now safe to return.
Take Mary and her child to Nazareth."
And once again, my Joseph led the way.

Jesus grew strong and kind.
He helped Joseph build with wood.
He read our holy books and learned of God.

When Jesus was twelve and nearly grown,
we traveled to the temple.
With God's people all around,
we climbed the steps and sang of God.
Jesus joined our song.

At the temple, we read and prayed and sang.
Then we left for home.
But Jesus was not with us!

I ran from friend to friend.
"Have you seen him? Have you seen my son?
I thought he was with you, or you.
He's not? . . . I'm scared!"

We hurried back to the temple and found him there.
He sat among the
greatest teachers of our land.
He listened. He taught!

"Son, why have you treated us like this?"
I cried. "You've frightened me to death."

"You looked for me?" he asked.
"You might have known that I'd be here.
This is my Father's house."

I held him close, and took him home.
But I remembered well the angels' song
about this Son of God.

23

And then he was a grown-up, a man.
He felt strong when he wrapped me in his arms.
He smelled of sweat and work.

One day we went to a wedding.
We laughed and sang for days.
But then our host looked worried.
"We've run out of wine," he told me.
"What will I do?
I'm out of money."

"Listen to him," I said,
and nodded toward my son.
"Fill these six jars with water," Jesus said.
"Now go and serve your guests."

I watched.
Water ran into the jars.
Wine poured out.

The slaves were shocked.
His disciples believed.
The wedding guests didn't know the difference.
And I? I knew that my son's
real work had just begun.

24

25

Hundreds and thousands of people followed Jesus.
He taught them about God, his Father.
He taught them the right way to live.
He made sick people well.
I followed too.

One day, more than four thousand
followed him into the hills.
For three days they listened and learned.
He saw that they were hungry.

"How much bread do you have?"
he asked his disciples.
"Five loaves," they answered.
"Fish?" he asked.
"Just a few," they shrugged.
"Feed the people," Jesus said.
They did, feeding all the thousands,
then gathered up the scraps,
seven baskets full.

What he said next made me cold all over.
"People hate me.
They will kill me.
It will happen soon."

It happened just as Jesus said.
I stood beneath his cross
the day that he died.

I heard his prayer,
"Father, forgive them.
They just don't understand."

And then he spoke to me.
"Dear mother," Jesus said.
"You need another son.
My friend John will care for you."
I felt John's arm around my back.

That night I sang again,
but now my song was moans of grief—
just as Simeon had foretold.
The son I loved was dead.

But Jesus didn't stay dead!
Three days later, my friends
rushed to my door.
"He's alive!" they said.
"He spoke to me," one said.
"The grave is empty," shouted another.
"Peter saw it too!"

"If God can die,
can God raise back to life?"
I wondered aloud.
This son of mine, God's Son, was alive again!
I gathered with my friends.

We saw him now and then.
He would come into our shuttered rooms
and speak of peace.

After forty days we gathered on a hill
and saw him lifted up to heaven.
My son, God's Son, returned to his Father God.

Ten days later, we gathered in a room
to pray and wait for something more—
a Comforter in his place,
just as Jesus told us.

A rushing wind tore through the room.
A flame of fire shone on each head.
Our voices spoke in languages
that we had never heard.
God's Spirit came with power.

A sound rose in my throat,
a song I'd never learned,
in words the angels sing.
I sang to God on high—
and people heard
of Jesus Christ
who lived
and died
and rose again
and lives on high
to save from sin.
Amen.